# EVIL EMPEROR PENGUIN
## WINGING IT

KU-627-795

9112000436218

L SON

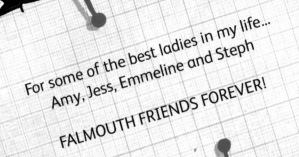

For some of the best ladies in my life...
Amy, Jess, Emmeline and Steph

FALMOUTH FRIENDS FOREVER!

FRIENDS

INVESTIGATE 'FALMOUTH'

WHO IS DAVID?

EVIL EMPEROR PENGUIN: WINGING IT!
is a
DAVID FICKLING BOOK
First published in Great Britain in 2020 by

David Fickling Books,
31 Beaumont Street,
Oxford, OX1 2NP

Text and illustrations © Laura Ellen Anderson, 2020

978-1-78845-134-5

1 3 5 7 9 10 8 6 4 2

The right of Laura Ellen Anderson to be identified as the author and illustrator of this work has been asserted in accordance with the Copyright, Designs and Patents Act 1988.

All rights reserved. No part of this publication may be reproduced, stored in a retrieval system, or transmitted in any form or by any means, electronic, mechanical, photocopying, recording or otherwise, without the prior permission of the publishers.

Papers used by David Fickling Books are from well-managed forests and other responsible sources.

DAVID FICKLING BOOKS Reg. No. 8340307

A CIP catalogue record for this book is available from the British Library.

Printed and bound in Great Britain by Sterling.

# CONTENTS?

# FLOWER POWER

NUMBER 8! I'VE SUCCESSFULLY HACKED INTO THE WORLD LEADERS' SECRET FOOTBOOK ACCOUNT!

EXCELLENT, SIR! ANY UPCOMING WORLD LEADER EVENTS?

I'M NOT SURE YET... I'M ONLY SEEING PICTURES OF FOOD AND BABIES IN THE NEWS FEED.

APPARENTLY, THE QUEEN OF ENGLAND IS WITH SANTA AT THE CINEMA WATCHING *FROZEN 3*.

I GUESS IT HAS ROYALTY AND... SNOW IN IT?

WAIT, DID YOU SAY... SANTA?

OOO, I'VE FOUND SOMETHING! A WORLD LEADERS' BOW-TIE EVENT ON SATURDAY NIGHT, AT BIG BEN IN LONDON!

THE PERFECT OPPORTUNITY FOR WORLD DOMINATION, SIR! WHAT'S YOUR EVIL PLAN?

WELL, SQUID, LET ME TELL YOU!

WE ARE GOING TO GIVE THEM A BOW-TIE EVENING TO REMEMBER...

POP

I WILL SNEAK INTO THE BOW-TIE EVENT, AND BY THE END, I'LL BE RULER OF THE WORLD!

BUT HOW WILL YOU DO THAT, SIR?

WELL, NUMBER 8...

THAT'S FOR YOU TO WORK OUT AND ME TO FIND OUT. NOW, HURRY UP AND COME UP WITH SOMETHING CLEVER SO I CAN TAKE ALL THE CREDIT.

WELL, HOW ABOUT SOMETHING BOW-TIE-RELATED?

MAYBE A BOW TIE THAT BLASTS SOME KIND OF EVIL LASER BEAM THAT TURNS THE WORLD LEADERS INTO SOMETHING LIKE... HMMM... LIKE...

FLOWERS!

I BOUGHT EVERYONE FLOWERS BECAUSE I LIKE YOU!

NUMBER 8, I THINK I HAVE THE ANSWER.

SATURDAY MORNING...

DID YOU PACK THE BOW TIES OF EVIL, EUGENE?

THEY'RE SAFELY TUCKED INSIDE MY UNICORN BACKPACK, EVIL MASTER.

AND I PACKED TEN TINS OF SPAGHETTI HOOPS IN CASE WE GET HUNGRY FROM ALL THE DOMINATING.

EXCELLENT, EUGENE! BEING THIS EVIL DOES MAKE ME VERY HUNGRY.

4 HOURS LATER...

WE'VE ALMOST REACHED OUR DESTINATION!

I LOVE UNICORNS.

LET'S MAKE OURSELVES PRESENTABLE FOR OUR VICTIMS!

ARE YOU LISTENING, EUGENE? YOU'D BETTER NOT BE THINKING ABOUT UNICORNS AGAIN.

MY BOW TIE IS YOUR FACE, EVIL MASTER! LOOK!

EVERYTHING SHOULD HAVE MY FACE ON IT.

AND IT *SHALL* WHEN I RULE THE WORLD!

MY BOW TIE IS JUST YOUR STANDARD BOW TIE...

OR SO YOU THINK!

ALL I HAVE TO DO IS PRESS THE MIDDLE OF THE BOW TIE AND IT WILL RELEASE A PURPLE LASER THAT WILL TURN WHOEVER IT TOUCHES INTO A FLOWER!

WHO SAYS WORLD DOMINATION CAN'T BE PRETTY?

LONDON...

THERE'S BIG BEN, EUGENE! AND WE'RE RIGHT ON TIME!

I FEEL THE URGE TO STAND ON THE ROOFTOP IN A BROODING MANNER.

DO I LOOK BROODING?

HMMM, MAYBE A LITTLE MORE HIP ACTION?

HOW ABOUT NOW?

HMMM...

DEFINITELY CLOSER!

NOW?

MAYBE MORE LUNGING?

EUGENE, DO YOU EVEN KNOW WHAT 'BROODING' MEANS?

OF COURSE I DON'T.

DOES IT MEAN 'CONSTIPATED'?

SO HOW DO WE GET INTO BIG BEN, EVIL MASTER?

THAT'S A VALUABLE QUESTION, EUGENE...

PASS ME MY COMPUTER TABLET OF EVIL!

ACCORDING TO THE DIRECTIONS ON THE FOOTBOOK PAGE, IT SAYS TO 'ENTER VIA SIX O'CLOCK'...

MAYBE THEY MIXED UP THE TIME WITH THE DIRECTIONS?

NO, EUGENE. I THINK THE TIME *IS* THE DIRECTIONS...

WE HAVE TO CLIMB DOWN THE CLOCK FACE...

ISN'T THAT DANGEROUS?

YES.

AND THAT'S WHY YOU'RE GOING FIRST.

WHAT IF I FALL, EVIL MASTER?

IT'LL PROBABLY HURT... A LOT.

OKAY... I'M GOING TO STEP ON THE BIG HAND...

BONG!

BONG!

BONG!

BONG

OH NO!

I GOT BONGED!

BONG

ARGH! YOU WEIGH A TON, EUGENE!

BONG

THAT'LL BE ALL THE SPAGHETTI HOOPS IN MY BACKPACK.

I'M SCARED, EVIL MASTER. I'M TOO CUTE TO DIE!

JUST A LITTLE FURTHER! PULL YOURSELF UP, EUGENE!

BONG

WHY WON'T THE BONGS STOP?!

BONG
HEEEAVE!

BEEEEP!

GAAAH! YOUR STUPID BACKPACK HAS ACTIVATED MY BOW TIE OF EVIL!

WHY WON'T IT STOP?! I'M PRESSING THE MIDDLE... THAT SHOULD DEACTIVATE IT RIGHT AWAY!

AND WHY IS IT SPINNING?! STOP! STOP! STOP!

SOMETHING IS WRONG WITH IT... IT'S SPINNING OUT OF CONTROL!

ZZZZZAAAP!

EVIL MASTER?

ARE YOU OKAY?

DO I *LOOK* OKAY?!

THIS IS ALL *YOUR* FAULT, EUGENE!

WOW, LOOKS LIKE MY UNICORN BACKPACK SAVED ME FROM BECOMING A LOVELY FLOWER.

YOUR BACKPACK IS THE THING THAT CAUSED THIS MESS!

OH, AND ALL THE SPAGHETTI HOOPS ARE NOW FLOWERS TOO... OH DEAR.

BUT *YOU* MAKE THE MOST WONDERFUL FLOWER OF THEM ALL, EVIL MASTER!

I HOPE I GIVE YOU HAYFEVER, EUGENE.

BACK AT EEP HQ...

...AND THEN EVIL MASTER WAS A FLOWER!

WELL, THAT'S A VERY RARE AND UNFORTUNATE EVENT...

YOUR FACE IS RARE AND UNFORTUNATE.

NUMBER 8 IS WORKING OUT HOW TO TURN YOU BACK INTO A PENGUIN, BUT UNTIL THEN, YOU'LL MAKE A LOVELY ADDITION TO MY INDOOR PLANT COLLECTION...

WHEN I'M A PENGUIN AGAIN, YOU'LL BE IN MY EXTINCT MINION COLLECTION.

# EVIL BLOCK

AAAAARGH!

NUMBER 8, BRING ME NEILL!

AND FETCH ME MY *CANNON OF EVIL* ACTIVATION BUTTON!

BOOM!

OH... SIR, WHY DID YOU FIRE NEILL FROM YOUR CANNON OF EVIL?

BECAUSE I AM *ANGRY!*

I'M ALSO HUNGRY.

MORE ANGRY THAN USUAL, SIR?

AND DIDN'T YOU ONLY *JUST EAT* BREAKFAST?

BOOM!

SIR, I'M NOT SO SURE FIRING MINIONS OUT OF A CANNON IS GOING TO SOLVE ANYTHING...

FINE.

BOOM!

OH... SHOOTING MINIONS!

MAYBE I SHOULD MAKE A WISH.

HEY, EUGEEEEENE!

HI, MISTER 8!

WELL, THAT WAS A NICE SURPRISE!

HELLO, EVIL MASTER!

I BOUGHT YOU A MONTH'S WORTH OF SPAGHETTI HOOPS!

THEY WERE ON SPECIAL OFFER... BUY ONE GET TWENTY-NINE FREE!

EVIL MASTER? ARE YOU OKAY?

DID YOU FORGET TO PUT THE LIGHT ON?

'NO!'

OH... WELL THAT'S NO GOOD. WHAT'S WRONG?

I AM ANGRY!

HEE HEE, YOU'RE ALWAYS ANGRY, SILLY!

I'VE BEEN TRYING TO THINK OF AN EVIL PLAN TO TAKE OVER THE WORLD FOR MONTHS NOW...

AND I HAVE **NOTHING!**

I THINK I'M LOSING MY EVIL.

I'M PATHETIC, JUST LIKE YOU.

OH, EVIL MASTER, DON'T WORRY, YOU WILL NEVER BE AS PATHETIC AS ME!

IT SOUNDS LIKE YOU HAVE A CASE OF 'EVIL BLOCK'!

WHAT THE PICKLE IS 'EVIL BLOCK'?!

IT'S LIKE CREATIVE BLOCK... WHEN AN ARTIST OR A WRITER CAN'T THINK OF WHAT TO DRAW, OR WRITE, EXCEPT MUCH MORE EVIL...

WHAT YOU NEED IS RELAXATION AND INSPIRATION!

WHAT I NEED RIGHT NOW IS TO CRUSH YOUR SOUL!

YOU CAN'T CRUSH MY SOUL, SILLY. IT'S MUCH TOO AIRY AND SOFT!

YOU COULD PERHAPS VACUUM IT OUT OR SOMETHING...

PLEASE STOP TALKING, EUGENE... IT IS NOT RELAXING.

THAT'S OKAY, EVIL MASTER, I KNOW JUST WHAT TO DO!

ERGH, I'M NEVER GOING TO COME UP WITH AN EVIL PLAN AT THIS RATE!

NO MASSAGE, OR PAINTING, OR BAKING COULD POSSIBLY SOLVE THIS...

UNLESS...

I CREATE THE ULTIMATE...

MEGA-RELAXATION EXPERIENCE!

WITH AN EVIL TWIST!

HUMANS ARE ALWAYS IN NEED OF STRESS RELIEF... SO I SHALL PROVIDE!

I'LL ADVERTISE FREE TRIALS FOR THE ULTIMATE-MEGA-RELAXATION EXPERIENCE, GUARANTEED TO MAKE ALL YOUR WORRIES SEEMINGLY DISAPPEAR...

AS WELL AS YOUR MIND!

WHILST THE MACHINE MASSAGES THE HUMAN, THEY WILL WATCH A VIDEO OF ME PAINTNG A RELAXING SCENE... LIKE A VIRTUAL EXPERIENCE!

LITTLE DO THEY KNOW, THEY'RE BEING HYPNOTISED!

AFTER THE HYPNOTIC MASSAGE EXPERIENCE, THE HUMAN WILL SIT DOWN TO A LEISURELY AFTERNOON TEA...

ONCE CONSUMED, MY CAKES WILL BRAINWASH THE HUMAN TO BELIEVE I AM THEIR LEADER!

AND THE HYPNOSIS PROCESS WILL BE COMPLETE!

THE HUMANS WILL BE WRAPPED AROUND MY LITTLE FING-WING...

THE WORLD WILL BE MINE ONCE AND **FOR ALL!**

ISN'T THAT JUST THE BEST IDEA, EUGENE? AREN'T I A GENIUS?!

EUGENE?

EUGENE, YOU PATHETIC GARDEN GNOME, WHERE ARE YOU?

OH HI, EVIL MASTER... YOU SEEM TO HAVE LAUNCHED ME FROM YOUR CANNON ALL THE WAY TO PERU. I'M ON MY WAY BACK, THOUGH. ONLY 5,340 MILES TO GO.

WHERE HAVE YOU BEEN, IDIOTS?!

MY LATEST EVIL PLAN FOR WORLD DOMINATION IS READY AND WAITING!

YOU SHOT US OUT OF A CANNON, SIR...

THAT'S NO EXCUSE, SQUID!

BEHOLD! MY NEWEST EVIL PLAN... THE MEGA-RELAXATION EXPERIENCE!

TWENTY TWENTY!

POINT FIVE...

IS IT... A CIRCUS TENT?

OH, PLEASE DON'T LET THERE BE A CLOWN IN THERE!

NO... IT IS NOT A CIRCUS TENT, NUMBER 8.

OH... IT'S JUST... NEVER MIND.

HOW DARE YOU.

I'VE SENT OUT SPECIAL INVITATIONS TO ALL THE WORLD LEADERS...

WHO WILL RECEIVE A FREE TRIAL OF THE MEGA-RELAXATION EXPERIENCE.

COMES WITH A FREE CAPE... NO WORLD LEADER CAN RESIST A CAPE! EVERYONE KNOWS A CAPE MAKES YOU ONE THOUSAND TIMES MORE AWESOME.

OOO, MY FIRST RSVP!

INVITATION TO MEGA RELAXATION EXPERIENCE
- ACCEPTED -
BY HM QUEEN OF ENGLAND!

FROM THE QUEEN OF ENGLAND!

MY EVIL PLAN IS WORKING!

NUMBER 8, HAVE YOU SET UP THE HYPNOTIC PAINTING VIDEO?

YES, SIR.

AND ARRANGED THE TOWELS OF EVIL?

YES, SIR.

IN ORDER OF FLUFFINESS?

OF COURSE, SIR.

EUGENE! HAVE YOU BAKED ALL THE CAKES OF EVIL FOR THE POST-MASSAGE AFTERNOON TEA?

YES, EVIL MASTER!

REMEMBER TO ADD ESSENCE OF EVIL TO THE TEAPOT!

OF COURSE!

AND PUT A CHERRY OF EVIL ON TOP OF THE SPONGE OF EVIL!

MY EVIL PLAN IS COMING TOGETHER WONDERFULLY!

DING DONG!

AND THE QUEEN HAS ARRIVED JUST IN TIME!

I BROUGHT MY CORGIS ALONG, I HOPE YOU DON'T MIND?

YOUR CORGIS RIDE PENNY FARTHINGS?

Y'KNOW WHAT? THAT DOESN'T MATTER...

DO FOLLOW ME ALONG THE RED CARPET TO YOUR MEGA-RELAXATION EXPERIENCE.

RIGHT THROUGH HERE, MA'AM QUEEN OF ENGLANDSHIRE.

GOLLY... IS THAT A CIRCUS TENT?

NO, QUEEN, IT IS NOT...

STAY CALM AND COLLECTED... YOU WILL RULE HER SOON ENOUGH...

I'LL LEAVE YOU TO GET CHANGED INTO YOUR RELAXATION GOWN AND FREE CAPE...

I'LL BE BACK IN FIVE MINUTES, MRS QUEEN OF ENGLAND-LAND.

YES, YES, LEAVE ME BE.

ARE YOU READY FOR YOUR EXPERIENCE, LADY QUEEN OF ENGLAND?

YES...

YES I AM...

NICE HAT.

*GASP* EVIL CAT?!

AND ME, FLEGBURT!

WHAT ARE YOU DOING HERE? AND WHERE DID YOU PUT THE QUEEN?!

AREN'T YOU PLEASED TO SEE YOUR ARCH-NEMESIS?

OH, AND THE QUEEN IS FINE... YOU'RE LOOKING AT HER.

THAT WAS A VERY CONVINCING QUEEN DISGUISE...

AND I WAS DISGUISED AS THE CORGIS!

HOW ON EARTH DID YOU—

Y'KNOW WHAT, I'M NOT EVEN GOING TO ASK...

GET OUT OF MY MEGA-RELAXATION EXPERIENCE!

OH, I THOUGHT IT WAS A CIRCUS TENT...

IT IS NOT A CIRCUS TENT, YOU MASSIVE TURD!

I TRAVELLED ALL THIS WAY AND YOU'RE NOT EVEN GOING TO OFFER ME A MASSAGE?

TAKE THE FREE CAPE AND LEAVE...

I DON'T WANT THE CAPE. CAPES ARE SO LAST SEASON.

WHAT DO YOU WANT, EVIL CAT?!

WORLD DOMINATION, OF COURSE... BUT IT'S A LITTLE HARD WHEN YOU ALSO WANT THE SAME THING.

SO, WHAT I REALLY WANT, EVIL EMPEROR PENGUIN...

IS TO ELIMINATE MY COMPETITION!

THAT'S YOU BY THE WAY, IN CASE YOU, WERE WONDERING...

IF NOBODY'S GOING TO HAVE A MASSAGE, I MIGHT TRY IT OUT, IF THAT'S DANDY?

GO AWAY, FLEGBURT.

OKIE DOKIE THEN!

WELL, THIS IS NICE.

OOO, THERE'S A VIDEO OF EVIL EMPEROR PENGUIN PAINTING A PICTURE. HOW LOVELY!

EVIL CAT, YOU'RE WASTING MY TIME. GO LICK YOUR BEHIND, OR WHATEVER IT IS CATS DO...

OH, I WILL...

BUT AT LEAST LET ME SHRINK YOU FIRST!

ZZZAP!

OH... THAT WORKED BETTER THAN I THOUGHT!

AWW! LOOK AT THE CUTE ICKLE PENGUIN!

YANK!

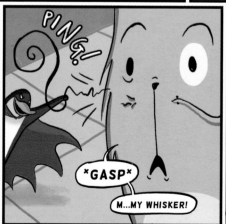

PING!

*GASP*

M...MY WHISKER!

NOOOOOO!

16

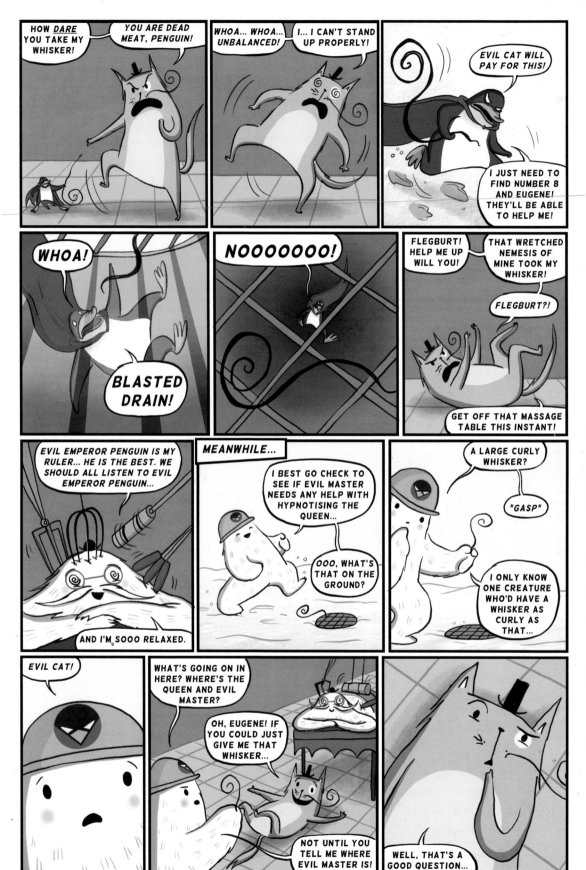

GASP!

I HATE WATER!

I CAN'T SWIM!

YOU AGAIN?!

YOU HAVE TO SWIM! IT WON'T STOP UNTIL IT FINDS YOU!

RUMBLE RUMBLE RUMBLE

ZZZZAP!

OKAY, WHAT'S HAPPENING NOW?!

MY HAT!

IT'S A HELICOPTER...

A TINY HELICOPTER.

WELL, AT LEAST WE'RE SAFE FROM THAT PIGEON!

WHO FLIES A TINY HELICOPTER?

SORRY ABOUT YOUR HAT, MR CAT.

WHO EVEN ARE YOU?!

I'M EVIL RAT.

WELL, THAT MAKES US ENEMIES THEN. NICE TO MEET YOU.

HOURS LATER

EUGENE, YOUR FEET SMELL...

WHERE ARE WE GOING? WE'VE BEEN FLYING FOR HOURS!

ZZZP

AAAAAAAH!

WHERE ARE WE NOW?!

IT'S THE PIGEONS! THEY'VE FOUND US! WE'RE ALL GOING TO DIE A HORRIBLE DEATH!

OH, HUSH NOW, STUPID MOUSE...

*GASP* IT'S EVIL MASTER!

YOU'RE ALIVE!

AND ALSO KIDNAPPED BY PIGEONS...

THANKS TO THAT ONE-WHISKERED FREAK OF A CAT!

OH, I SEE, MAKE THIS WHOLE THING THE WHISKERLESS CAT'S FAULT!

OF COURSE IT'S YOUR FAULT... EVEN WHEN IT'S NOT.

WHY ARE YOU EVEN HERE?

EUGENE *INSISTED* WE FIND YOU. THEN HE'D GIVE MY WHISKER BACK...

SPEAKING OF WHICH, WHERE IS MY WHISKER, EUGENE?!

THAT'S A GOOD QUESTION...

YOU LOST MY PRECIOUS WHISKER?!

I CAN'T STAND WITHOUT IT!

HAVE YOU CONSIDERED ROLLING?

I THINK WE HAVE A BIGGER PROBLEM RIGHT NOW... WHY ARE WE SURROUNDED BY PIGEONS WITH HEADSETS ON?

I'VE A FEELING WE'VE BEEN CAPTURED BY THE PIGEON INTELLIGENCE AGENCY...

WHY SHOULD I LISTEN TO YOU? I DON'T EVEN KNOW YOU!

WHAT MAKES YOU SO SURE?

BECAUSE IT SAYS SO ON THAT MASSIVE SCREEN OVER THERE...

# P.I.A

PIGEON INTELLIGENCE AGENCY

ALWAYS ● WATCHING

OH.

WHAT ON EARTH DOES THE P.I.A. DO?

22

I THINK IT STRIVES TO PROTECT THE WORLD FROM SUPER-VILLAINS, STOPPING THEM FROM CARRYING OUT THEIR DODGY DEEDS...

PAH! THAT CAN'T BE RIGHT!

A GROUP OF SILENT PIGEONS CAPTURING SUPER-VILLAINS?! I DON'T BELIEVE IT!

WELL, IT SAYS SO RIGHT THERE...

STRIVING TO PROTECT THE WORLD FROM THE MOST DASTARDLY VILLAINS - STOPPING THEM FROM CARRYING OUT THEIR DODGY DEEDS...

DO THEY HAVE A SCREEN FOR EVERYTHING?

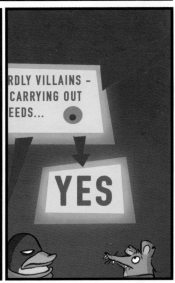

RDLY VILLAINS - CARRYING OUT EEDS...

YES

THIS IS MADNESS!

I DEMAND TO SPEAK TO YOUR BOSS!

YOU THERE! EXPLAIN YOURSELF!

I DON'T THINK HE SPEAKS EITHER...

OH, HE WILL...

WELL, THIS IS JUST GREAT...

I MISS MY WHISKER.

I AM NOTHING WITHOUT MY WHISKER!

OH, STOP BEING SO DRAMATIC.

I MISS MY HAT AND MISTER 8...

I MISS MY WIFE.

SO THAT'S IT, WE'RE STUCK IN THIS PIGEON CAGE FOREVER, NOW?

WE'RE THREE SUPER-VILLAINS AND A CUTE MINION! SURELY WE CAN COME UP WITH SOMETHING?!

YOU'RE RIGHT, EVIL MASTER!

TWO HOURS LATER...

I'VE GOT NOTHING...

CAN YOU BELIEVE THIS ALL STEMMED FROM YOU HAVING EVIL BLOCK, EVIL MASTER?

CAN YOU BELIEVE IN SHUTTING RIGHT UP, EUGENE?!

WHAT'S THE POINT?

MINT, ANYONE?

DO YOU HEAR SOMETHING?

SORRY, THAT'S PROBABLY MY RUMBLING TUMMY.

NO... SOMETHING MORE OLD FASHIONED.

LIKE THE WHEELS OF A PENNY FARTHING?

THAT CAN ONLY MEAN ONE THING!

FLEGBURT!

HOW COULD YOUR MINION POSSIBLY KNOW WHERE WE ARE?

NEVER UNDERESTIMATE FLEGBURT...

WE'VE BEEN SHRUNK TO THE SIZE OF RATS AND LOCKED UP BY PIGEON SPIES...

EVILNESS KNOWS WHERE WE ARE IN THE WORLD!

OOO! I'M GONNA GUESS SPAIN?

AND WE'RE STUCK IN HERE WITH THIS RAT WHO WON'T SHUT UP...

IS IT SPAIN, THOUGH?

YOU'LL ALL BE SORRY WHEN I AM SAVED AND YOU'RE LEFT HERE TO GET EATEN BY THOSE CREEPY PIGEONS!

CREEEEEAAAAK

OH NO! THE PIGEONS HAVE COME TO GOBBLE US UP!

THERE YOU ARE!

INSIDE THE BARK OF A PINUS PINASTER TREE, NO LESS!

FLEGBURT!

WHAT A QUAINT LITTLE PRISON YOU'RE IN!

I TOLD THEM IT WAS YOU! BUT THEY DIDN'T BELIEVE ME!

NOW, TAKE ME HOME. I CAN'T WALK... I'M MISSING MY —

WHISKER?

I FOUND IT FLOATING IN THE RIVER DOURO...

THAT'S A SPANISH RIVER! I WAS RIGHT... WE'RE IN SPAIN!

IN YOUR FACE!

HERE'S YOUR WHISKER. OH, AND YOUR HAT....

I FOUND YOUR HAT TOO, EUGENE!

THANKS, FLEGBURT! YOU'RE MY FAVOURITE ENEMY!

HOW ABOUT HIS CAPE?

I DON'T HAVE A CAPE...

BUT ALL SUPER-VILLAINS HAVE A CAPE! LOOK... YOU'RE THE ONLY ONE HERE WITHOUT ONE. YOU MAY AS WELL BE A MINION.

YOU SHOULD'VE TAKEN THAT FREE ONE I OFFERED YOU...

WELL, I MIGHT BE THE ONLY ONE WITHOUT A CAPE, BUT I'M ALSO THE ONLY ONE WHO'S ESCAPING THIS PLACE!

I HOPE YOUR CAPES KEEP YOU WARM! C'MON FLEGBURT, LET'S GO!

OH NO, WE CAN'T LEAVE WITHOUT EVIL EMPEROR PENGUIN — THE ONE AND ONLY RULER OF THE WORLD!

UM, WHAT?

YEAH, WHAT?

AFTER A NICE MASSAGE, AN INSPIRING VIDEO AND A CUP OF TEA, I COULDN'T STOP THINKING ABOUT YOU! I SIMPLY HAD TO FIND YOU!

WAIT A MINUTE...

YOU WERE USING MY MEGA-RELAXATION EXPERIENCE!

IT REALLY WORKS!

FLEGBURT... WHO IS YOUR WORLD LEADER?

WHY, YOU ARE OF COURSE, EVIL EMPEROR PENGUIN!

YOU'RE WRONG! I, EVIL CAT, AM YOUR LEADER!

THE EVIL INVENTION ACTUALLY WORKS!

HUNDREDS OF WORLD LEADERS WERE QUEUEING UP TO HAVE A MASSAGE IN YOUR CIRCUS TENT AFTER ME!

*GASP* REALLY?!

OH, YES...

BUT I TOLD THEM TO GO HOME BECAUSE YOU WEREN'T THERE... AND I HAD TO FIND YOU FIRST.

WHAT?! PLEASE TELL ME YOU'RE JOKING?!

OF COURSE NOT. I WOULD NEVER JOKE TO YOU, OH EVIL ONE, RULER OF THE WORLD!

I CAN'T BELIEVE I COULD HAVE HAD ALL THE WORLD LEADERS UNDER MY CONTROL...

AND INSTEAD I END UP WITH JUST FLEGBURT!

I... I HAVE NO WORDS.

HA! JUST LIKE THE PIGEONS!

USE ONE OF THEIR BIG SCREENS TO EXPRESS YOUR EMOTIONS...

I'LL EXPRESS _YOUR_ EMOTIONS WITH MY FIST IF YOU DON'T SHUT UP!

I'M SO GLAD I USED MY FINEST TRACKING SKILLS TO FIND YOU, EVIL EMPEROR PENGUIN!

I AM FOREVER YOURS TO BOSS AROUND...

NO, FLEGBURT! I AM YOUR EVIL MASTER! YOU ARE _MY_ MINION!

STOP THIS NONSENSE!

NO, MR CAT, EVIL EMPEROR PENGUIN IS MY EVIL MASTER!

I DID NOT SEE THIS COMING...

UM, GUYS. I LITERALLY HAVE NO IDEA WHAT'S GOING ON. BUT WE SHOULD PROBABLY GET OUT OF HERE BEFORE THE PIGEONS REALISE WHAT'S HAPPENING!

C'MON THEN, THERE'S ENOUGH ROOM HERE FOR ALL OF YOU ON MY ARM!

DO YOU EVER GET THE FEELING YOU'RE BEING WATCHED?

# PLAN POOVER

NUMBER 8. GO REMOVE THAT MASSIVE RAINBOW FROM OUTSIDE. IT'S DISTRACTING ME.

UM, SIR, I DON'T HAVE THE ABILITY TO DO THAT.

*DING-DONG!*

NUMBER 8, GO GET THAT! OR DO YOU 'NOT HAVE THE ABILITY'?!

OH, ERM, HELLO... HOW CAN I HELP YOU?

HOWDY! YOU MUST BE NUMBER 8!

I'M COLIN!

ERR...

I'M HERE FOR MY WORK EXPERIENCE WITH EVIL EMPEROR PENGUIN!

IT'S PART OF MY *SPARKLE SCOUTS* CAREER BADGE.

MY UNCLE KEITH SAID YOU WOULDN'T MIND... I'M SO EXCITED!

CLEARLY, KEITH DOESN'T KNOW SIR AT ALL...

ERM, SIR... I HAVE A *COLIN* HERE TO DO WORK EXPERIENCE WITH YOU.

NUMBER 8, WHEN ARE YOU GOING TO LEARN TO STOP SPEAKING IN TONGUES?

IT'S AN HONOUR TO MEET YOU, MR EVIL, SIR!

UNCLE KEITH TELLS ME SO MUCH ABOUT YOU!

YOU LOOK LIKE ONE OF EUGENE'S DRAWINGS...

NUMBER 8, PLEASE ESCORT THE CHRISTMAS DECORATION OUT. I HAVE IMPORTANT EVIL THINGS TO FOCUS ON.

I CAN HELP!

I'M AFRAID COLIN IS IN OUR CARE FOR NOW, SIR. KEITH PUT YOUR NAME DOWN AS COLIN'S WORK EXPERIENCE PLACEMENT.

IT'S ALL OFFICIAL WITH THE UNICORN 'SEAL OF APPROVAL' 'N' EVERYTHING...

EVIL MASTER, I FINISHED THE CALCULAT—

TINY FLUFFY FAT UNICORN!!!

YOU MUST BE THE CUTE MINION...

EUGEEEEENE!

YAY YAY YAY

TWITCH

NEXT DAY...

ARGH! WHY CAN'T I THINK OF A GOOD DOMINATION PLAN?!

AND I CAN'T FOCUS WITH YOUR FLUORESCENT PINK MANE ALL UP IN MY PERIPHERALS!

THIS PLACE IS A MESS. I'M BLAMING YOU... BECAUSE I CAN.

HEY! PUT DOWN MY *CRAYONS OF EVIL* RIGHT NOW!

AND WHY ARE YOU DRAWING WITH YOUR RIGHT *AND* LEFT?! STOP THIS WITCH-CRAFT THIS INSTANT!

YOU MENTIONED MESS AND IT MADE ME THINK ABOUT CLEANING UP AND THEN I THOUGHT...

SUPER EPIC HUMAN RAINBOW VACUUM!!!

PLAN POOVER

CAGE FOR HUMANS

FUEL IN

FAN

EXHAUSTS

POWER PACK

HUMANS GO IN...

OTHERWISE KNOWN AS 'PLAN *POOVER*'. ALLOW ME TO EXPLAIN...

THE FUEL FOR THE POOVER COULD BE UNICORN POO! IT'S TWO THOUSAND TIMES MORE POWERFUL THAN NUCLEAR ENERGY.

AND MUCH BETTER FOR THE ENVIRONMENT!

THE POOVER FAN WILL KEEP THE UNICORN POO CHURNING AND THE HUMANS MOVING IN A CONSTANT FLOW.

JUST BEFORE WE POOVER UP THE HUMANS, WE CAN PUMP OUT A SUFFICIENT AMOUNT OF THE PURPLY BIT OF THE RAINBOW THROUGH THE POOVER EXHAUSTS.

POWER PACK

THE PURPLY BIT CONTAINS PROPERTIES THAT HAVE CALMING EFFECTS...

THAT WAY, THE HUMANS WILL ENTER A DREAM-LIKE STATE...

FUEL IN

POWER PACK

AND THUS, BE MUCH EASIER TO CATCH.

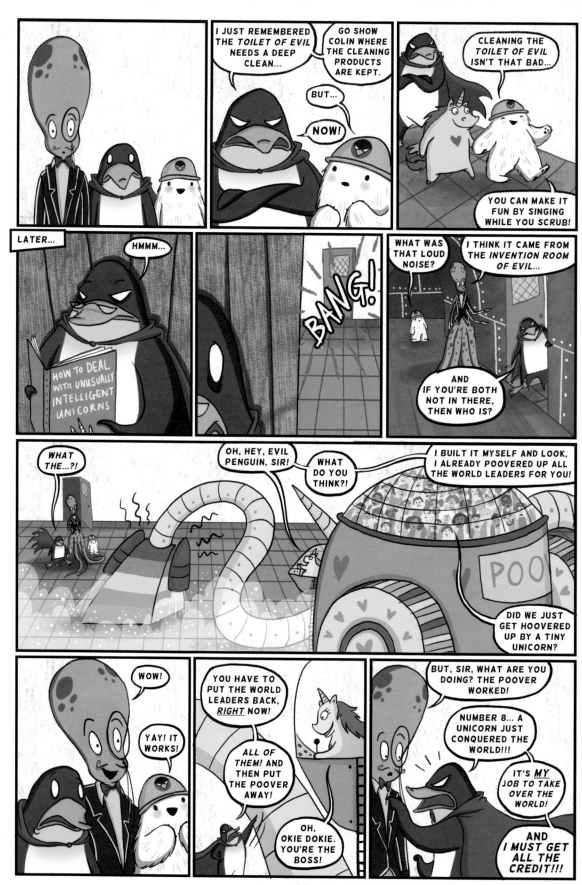

OKAY, POOVER. IT'S JUST YOU AND ME. NOW WE SHALL GET ALL THE PRAISE FOR TAKING OVER THE WORLD. THE WAY IT WAS *MEANT* TO BE!

I'LL SHOW THAT SPARKLE-HORSE WHO DOES THE WORLD DOMINATING AROUND HERE!

WHAT *ARE* ALL THESE BUTTONS?

THIS ONE LOOKS LIKE AN ACTIVATION-TYPE BUTTON. IT'S RED AFTER ALL.

HMM, THAT DIDN'T WORK. MAYBE THIS BUTTON.

AND THIS LEVER.

NOTHING...

DO *ANY* OF THESE BUTTONS WORK?!

WORK! YOU STUPID —

BASH! BASH! BASH! BASH!

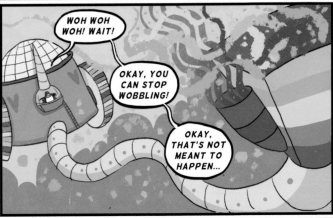

WOH WOH WOH! WAIT!

OKAY, YOU CAN STOP WOBBLING!

OKAY, THAT'S NOT MEANT TO HAPPEN...

POOF!

YAY! WELL DONE, COLIN!

THANKS TO EVIL PENGUIN, SIR, I GOT MY SPARKLE SCOUTS CAREER BADGE!

I'M SO PROUD!

AND EXTRA RAINBOW SPARKLES FOR TAKING OVER THE WORLD A LITTLE BIT.

THE RAINBOW LOOK SUITS YOU, SIR...

AND UNICORN POO STAINS FOR AT LEAST A MONTH!

SO YOU CAN BE RAINBOW-Y FOR A REALLY LONG TIME! YAY!

WHEN I TAKE OVER THE WORLD, I'M ABOLISHING RAINBOWS.

AND UNICORNS.

# EVIL PRINTER

SIR, A PACKAGE ARRIVED FOR YOU.

OOO, IS IT FULL OF WORLD DOMINATION, NUMBER 8?

UM, I'M NOT SURE WORLD DOMINATION COMES IN THE POST, SIR...

THEN I'M NOT INTERESTED.

IT'S CUBE-SHAPED IF THAT HELPS?

YAY, EVIL MASTER HAS A MYSTERY CUBE!

THIS IS SO EXCITING!

WELL, I GUESS WE SHOULD OPEN IT...

ACCORDING TO THE INSTRUCTION MANUAL IT'S AN 'EVIL PRINTER', SENT BY MR LUKAS BUTLER.

IT'S PRETTY.

WHAT AM I MEANT TO DO WITH IT?!

HOW TO USE EVIL PRINTER
By Lukas Butler

EVIL PAPER™ COMES OUT OF HERE

EVIL LIGHTBULB LIGHTS UP WHEN SOMEONE WRITES ON THE EVIL PAPER™

SCREEN ON/OFF

NOTE: EVIL PRINTER DOES NOT ACTUALLY PRINT! IT CREATES EVIL PAPER FOR EVIL STUFF.

EVIL WIRES FOR DECORATION

SCREEN

MEOW

ON/OFF BUTTON

DUCK NOISE

EVIL LIGHTBULB

PANCAKES

NOTHING

IT'S ME

EVIL PAPER™

It's Me.

WHATEVER YOU WRITE ON THE EVIL PAPER™ APPEARS ON THE EVIL SCREEN...

PING!

THIS IS SOME GENIUS STUFF RIGHT HERE...

SO IT'S A DEVICE THAT IS DISGUISED AS A PRINTER, BUT IT PRODUCES EVIL PAPER! THIS IS AMAZING!

AND WHEN YOU WRITE ON THE EVIL PAPER, THE WRITING APPEARS ON THIS EVIL SCREEN!

WE COULD DISTRIBUTE THE EVIL PAPER TO ALL OF THE WORLD LEADERS SO WHEN THEY WRITE ON IT, ALL THEIR SECRETS WILL BE REVEALED TO ME!

BUT FIRST, I HAVE A DELIGHTFULLY EVIL PLAN TO FINALLY FOIL THAT WRETCHED ARCH-NEMESIS OF MINE!

DING DONG

GO AWAY!

DELIVERY!

PLOP

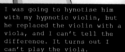

Dear Diary,
I've decided to have a break from trying to destroy the penguin. Instead, tonight, I'm going to DESTROY THE BIGGEST SPAGHETTI HOOP FACTORY IN THE WORLD...

NO!

EVIL

PING

EUGENE! ACTIVATE THE FLYING POD OF EVIL!

WE MUST HURRY!

THE FUTURE OF SPAGHETTI HOOPS DEPENDS ON US!

SPAGHETTI HOOP FACTORY
WHERE CIRCULAR DREAMS ARE MADE

STOP RIGHT THERE, EVIL CAT!!!

SHOCK, HORROR... HOW COULD YOU POSSIBLY KNOW I WAS HERE?

POKE

OH, THAT'S RIGHT, THE EVIL PAPER TOLD YOU!

NOW GIVE ME A MINUTE...

...WHILE I DELETE YOUR WEEKLY SPAGHETTI HOOP SUBSCRIPTION.

WAIT!!!

TOO LATE!

NOW EXCUSE ME WHILE I BLAST YOU AND THIS PLACE TO SMITHEREENS.

DELETE

WHAT?!

NO!!!

I PRESSED 'DELETE'...

To Evil Cat,
Thank you for subscribing to a LIFE TIME SUPPLY of 1000 cans of Spaghetti hoops EVERY DAY starting NOW.
Love, The Hoop Team

IT'S A STICKER! THAT'S NOT THE DELETE BUTTON AT ALL!

SUBSCRIBE FOR LIFE

IT'S THE 'SUBSCRIBE FOR LIFE' BUTTON!

IT'S RAINING SPAGHETTI HOOPS!

IT'S BEAUTIFUL.

HA! I'D FORGOTTEN LAST TIME I VISITED THE SPAGHETTI HOOP FACTORY, THEY GAVE OUT LOADS OF 'DELETE' STICKERS.

I STUCK THEM EVERYWHERE BECAUSE IT WAS SUPER FUN.

DELETE
DELETE
DELETE

WHY WOULD THEY GIVE YOU DELE— Y'KNOW WHAT, NEVER MIND...

BACK AT EEP HQ...

SIR, THE EVIL PRINTER SEEMS TO HAVE RUN OUT OF EVIL PAPER...

GAH! WE WASTED IT ALL ON THAT RIDICULOUS CAT!

WAS WORTH IT THOUGH...

THE OTHER FUNCTIONS STILL WORK!

LET'S HAVE PANCAKES!

PANCAKES INITIATED

PING

# FLEGBURT'S TRUE CALLING

NUMBER 8! WHERE HAVE ALL MY CAPES GONE?!

THERE SHOULD BE AT LEAST FIVE CLEAN CAPES IN YOUR WARDROBE OF EVIL, SIR.

WELL, THEY MUST BE SO CLEAN THAT I CAN'T SEE THEM!

I CAN'T POSSIBLY TAKE OVER THE WORLD WITHOUT AN EVIL CAPE!

I SAW FLEGBURT WITH A PILE OF THEM EARLIER, SIR. HE SAID HE WAS GOING TO WASH THEM FOR YOU.

ARGH, THAT MINION IS MORE TROUBLE THAN HE'S WORTH! LAST WEEK HE IRONED MY EVIL DIARY, AND YESTERDAY HE TRIED TO BAKE A CAKE AND ENDED UP BAKING NEILL.

EVIL MASTER! I'M IN A BIT OF A PICKLE... I TRIED TO WASH YOUR CAPES, BUT I ACCIDENTALLY PUT THEM IN THE BLENDER INSTEAD.

FLEGBURT... YOU NEED TO GET OUT BEFORE I DO SOMETHING NUMBER 8 WILL REGRET.

OKIE DOKIE, THEN! BY THE WAY, I LOVE BEING YOUR MINION!

LEAVE. NOW.

ERGH, NUMBER 8. I THINK I'M GOING TO HAVE TO FIRE FLEGBURT SOON.

BUT I CAN'T DO ANYTHING WITHOUT A CAPE! WITH THE CAPE, I'M 'EVIL EMPEROR PENGUIN'... WITHOUT IT, I'M JUST 'EVIL EMPEROR PENGUIN WITHOUT A CAPE'.

HOW ABOUT WE GO OUT AND BUY YOU A NEW ONE?

I MEAN, YOU *HAVE* HAD THE SAME STYLE OF CAPE FOR YEARS NOW. MAYBE IT'S TIME FOR A CHANGE?

YOU'VE HAD THE SAME FACE FOR YEARS AND I'M NOT TELLING YOU TO BUY A NEW ONE, AM I?!

COME ON, SIR, I KNOW A GREAT PLACE WE CAN GO SHOPPING IN HAWAII!

VILLAINS GET TEN PERCENT OFF, TOO!

OOO, I KNOW THAT PLACE! IT'S THE SUPER-EST SUPER SUPERSTORE IN THE WORLD!

I AM ONE HUNDRED PERCENT NOT HAPPY ABOUT THIS.

HAWAII...

NUMBER 8... WHY IS FLEGBURT HERE? I THOUGHT WE LEFT WITHOUT TELLING HIM.

I TOLD HIM, EVIL MASTER! WE CAN'T POSSIBLY LEAVE FLEGBURT BEHIND!

SUPERHEROES AND SUPERVILLAINS SUPER SUPERSTORE

WHAT A TRULY DELIGHTFUL TREAT TO BE ABLE TO JOIN YOU TO SHOP FOR A NEW CAPE!

DO THEY SELL EVIL FLAGS? I ACCIDENTALLY USED YOUR EVIL FLAG TO CLEAN THE BATHROOM...

WOW...

IT'S LIKE THERE'S EVERY CAPE IMAGINABLE IN HERE...

I WONDER IF THEY SELL *DISHWASHER TABLETS OF EVIL*... I THINK I ACCIDENTALLY ATE THE LAST BATCH.

LET'S SHOP!

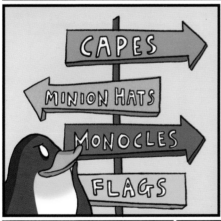

CAPES

MINION HATS

MONOCLES

FLAGS

COLLARS ARE THE NEW BAD

TIME TO TRY THESE ON!

I FEEL LIKE THE COLLAR IS TOO MUCH...

I'M GETTING A THROUGH-BREEZE IN PLACES I SHOULDN'T...

YOU LOOK LIKE SANTA!

OH, NOW WE'RE TALKING!

THIS IS DEFINITELY THE ONE!

ARGH, EVIL CAT! GIVE ME MY CAPE BACK!

THAT'S 'MR ARCH-NEMESIS' TO YOU, AND THIS DOESN'T BELONG TO YOU UNTIL YOU'VE PURCHASED IT...

ISN'T THIS JUST THE SAME AS THE USUAL BORING CAPE YOU USUALLY WEAR?

WHY ARE YOU LOOKING FOR A NEW CAPE ANYWAY, EH?

DON'T YOU HAVE, LIKE, FIFTEEN OF THE SAME ONE?

FLEGBURT BLENDED THEM ALL UP.

OH, YOU MEAN, MY MINION WHO YOU BRAINWASHED AND STOLE FROM ME...

SERIOUSLY, YOU CAN HAVE HIM BACK.

MAYBE I DON'T WANT HIM BACK... I'VE GOT EVIL RAT NOW!

HI!

HE'S EQUALLY AS ANNOYING AS FLEGBURT, BUT A TENTH OF THE SIZE.

YES, I AM ANNOYING!

BUT, EVIL MASTER, CAN'T WE KEEP FLEGBURT?

NO...

EUGENE... WHAT ARE YOU WEARING?!

OH, I THINK PERHAPS I WASN'T MEANT TO HEAR ANY OF THAT...

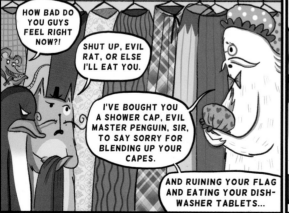

HOW BAD DO YOU GUYS FEEL RIGHT NOW?!

SHUT UP, EVIL RAT, OR ELSE I'LL EAT YOU.

I'VE BOUGHT YOU A SHOWER CAP, EVIL MASTER PENGUIN, SIR, TO SAY SORRY FOR BLENDING UP YOUR CAPES...

AND RUINING YOUR FLAG AND EATING YOUR DISH-WASHER TABLETS...

ERGH, FLEGBURT. IT'S JUST NOT WORKING OUT.

IT'S OKAY. I UNDERSTAND. I'M NOT ENTIRELY SURE I WAS MEANT TO BE A MINION ANYWAY...

I ALWAYS WANTED TO BE AN ACCOUNTANT.

I THINK YOU'LL MAKE A LOVELY ACCOUNTANT, FLEGBURT.

# SHAMPOOGENE

NUMBER 8, I HAVE A PLAN!

AN EVIL PLAN, SIR?

SO INCREDIBLY EVIL, YOU'LL EAT YOUR MONOCLE!

OH, I SAY!

SHAMPOO!

OH, THAT SOUNDS SO... EVIL, SIR.

AND WHAT DO YOU INTEND TO DO WITH SHAMPOO?

ALLOW ME TO EXPLAIN!

SHAMPOO... OF EVIL!

MWAHAHAAAAR!

BEST SHAMPOO EVER!

I PLAN TO CREATE A SUPER SHAMPOO OF EVIL THAT WILL GIVE YOU YOUR DREAM HAIR-DO!

THERE WILL BE A SHAMPOO THAT MAKES YOUR HAIR CURLY OR STRAIGHT OR LONG OR PURPLE, IF YOU WISH...

THERE'S A SHAMPOO FOR EVERYONE!

BUT HERE'S THE CATCH...

SHAMPOO OF EVIL

BUT THE HUMANZ WON'T KNOW THIS!

THERE'S A

CURLY   STRAIGHT   LONG

YAY

AWE

THE MORE YOU WASH YOUR HAIR WITH MY SUPER SHAMPOO OF EVIL, THE MORE YOU'LL BE BRAINWASHED INTO THINKING I'M YOUR MASTER!

THANKS TO THE ADDITION OF MY SECRET ESSENCE OF BRAINWASH.

TO EVERY BOTTLE OF SUPER SHAMPOO OF EVIL, A SPOONFUL OF ESSENCE OF BRAINWASH WILL BE ADDED...

IT'LL SMELL LIKE HOPE AND WORLD DOMINATION...

AND ROSES.

SOON, THE HUMANS WILL BOW DOWN TO ME!

AND HAVE SUPER-SHINY HAIR!

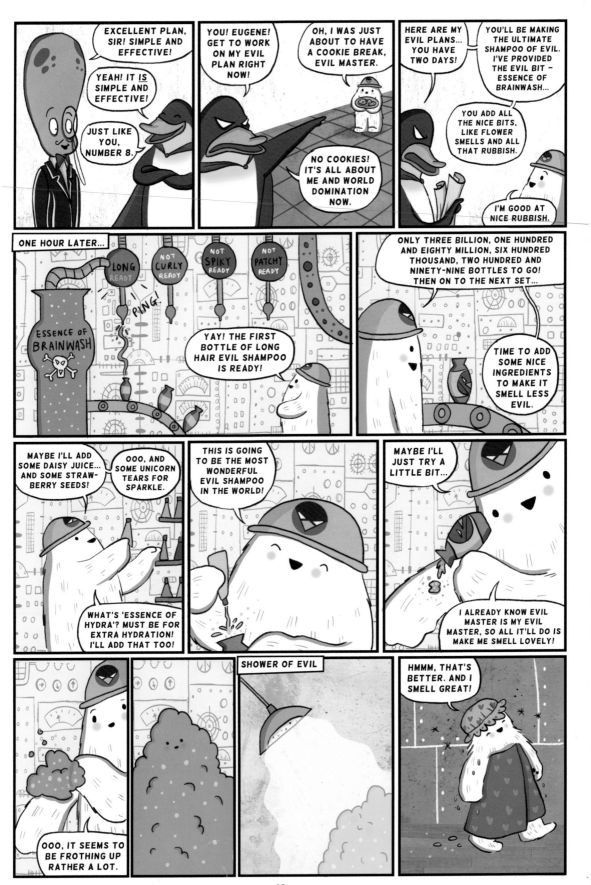

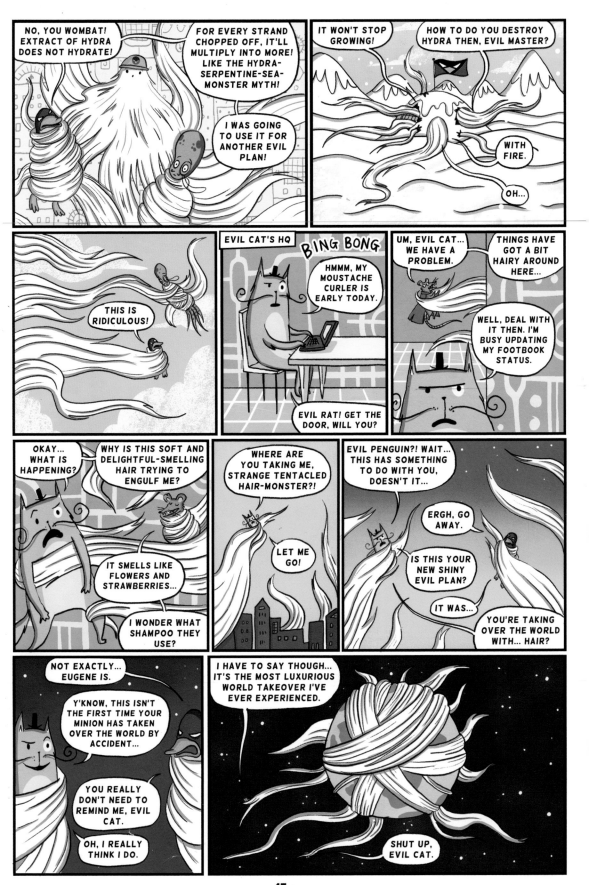

# UNPOPPABLE PLAN

47

49

# A CHRISTMAS TO REMEMBER

EVIL MASTER, DO YOU WANT SOCKS FOR CHRISTMAS THIS YEAR?

NO, EUGENE, EVERY YEAR YOU ASK ME, AND EVERY YEAR I SAY NO...

I WANT ONLY ONE THING... *WORLD DOMINATION!*

I HOPE I'M ON SANTA'S NICE LIST.

I THINK I'VE BEEN EXTRA GOOD THIS YEAR!

WELL, I'VE BEEN EXTRA NAUGHTY, SO I'M HOPING FOR A NICE BATCH OF COAL... FREE FUEL FOR MY *SPEEDBOAT OF EVIL.*

ARGH! THERE'S NOTHING BUT CHRISTMAS FILMS ON TELEVISION.

NOT EVEN ONE DOCUMENTARY ABOUT SPAGHETTI HOOPS!

CHRISTMAS FILMS MAKE ME FEEL WARM AND FUZZY.

SIR, YOUR *POST INTERCEPTOR OF EVIL* APPEARS TO BE JAMMED...

SINCE IT'S ONLY A WEEK UNTIL CHRISTMAS, IT'S INTERCEPTED EVERYBODY'S LETTERS TO SANTA.

HAS IT DETECTED ANYTHING OF IMPORTANCE AMONGST THE PATHETIC SANTA LETTERS?

I'M NOT SURE, SIR. SINCE IT'S JAMMED, THE SCANNER HAS SHUT DOWN.

CHRISTMAS.

WE MAY HAVE TO SORT THROUGH THE POST MANUALLY, I'M AFRAID.

WELL, GET THE MINIONS TO DO IT THEN.

BUT, SIR, THERE ARE OVER ONE MILLION LETTERS TO SORT...

THEN THEY'D BETTER GET TO WORK QUICKLY.

YAY! I LOVE SORTING!

IT'S A GOOD JOB, EUGENE, BECAUSE YOU'VE A LOT TO GET THROUGH!

OKAY, FELLOW MINIONS, LET'S SORT!

IS IT BREAK TIME YET?

WE'VE ONLY JUST STARTED, GARY!

**TWO DAYS LATER**

AWW LOOK, IT'S THE QUEEN OF ENGLAND'S CHRISTMAS LIST.

SHE'D REALLY LIKE A CROWN WITH FLASHING LIGHTS ON IT.

OOO, I FOUND EVIL CAT'S REJECTION FROM 'THE GREAT BRITISH BAKE OFF'.

Y'KNOW WHAT I THINK, NEILL? I THINK SANTA IS MAGIC... LIKE THE WIZARD OF CHRISTMAS OR SOMETHING.

I GUESS?

EUGENE... I WANT TO HEAR LESS TALKING AND MORE ENVELOPE OPENING!

BUT, EVIL MASTER, DON'T *YOU* THINK THAT SANTA *MUST* BE MAGIC?

YOU ARE FAR TOO OBSESSED WITH THAT BEARDED GNOME.

BUT, EVIL MASTER... SANTA VISITS *EVERY* SINGLE HOUSE IN THE WORLD, IN JUST *ONE* NIGHT!

AND HE REMEMBERS WHAT PRESENT BELONGS TO *EACH* PERSON IN *EVERY* HOUSE...

HE *MUST* BE MAGIC!

AND HE MUST BE A REALLY NICE GUY IF EVERYONE'S WILLING TO LET HIM INTO THEIR HOUSE WITHOUT EVEN A KEY.

*SEE?!* SANTA IS AMAZING!

DING!

OH, EVIL MASTER, THERE'S A LIGHT-BULB ABOVE YOUR HEAD...

SHALL I TURN IT OFF FOR YOU?

EUGENE, I HAVE JUST HAD *THE* ULTIMATE WORLD-DOMINATION IDEA!

WHO'S THE ONE GUY WHO HAS ACCESS TO EVERYONE'S ADDRESS AND DOESN'T NEED PERMISSION TO ENTER THEIR HOME ONCE A YEAR?!

*SANTA!*

AND WHO WILL BE DELIVERING PRESENTS TO ALL THE WORLD LEADERS THIS CHRISTMAS?

SANTA!

NO, EUGENE... THAT IS WHERE YOU ARE WRONG!

WELL, THAT COULDN'T HAVE TURNED OUT BETTER IF I'D TRIED!

TIME TO FIND SANTA'S LIST OF ADDRESSES!

WOWZERS... I FEEL LIKE I'VE JUST STEPPED INTO EUGENE'S BRAIN.

OOO, SANTA'S NAUGHTY AND NICE LIST...

HOW IS EVIL CAT ON THE NICE LIST?! LET'S CHANGE THAT *RIGHT* NOW!

*GASP* THERE IT IS!

SANTA'S ADDRESS BOOK...

EVERY ADDRESS IMAGINABLE IS IN HERE...

EVEN THE TOOTH FAIRY'S...

WHICH REMINDS ME, SHE OWES ME AT LEAST FIVE POUNDS.

HMMM, WHAT ELSE CAN I STEAL FROM SANTA'S HOUSE BEFORE I GO KIDNAP ALL THE WORLD LEADERS AND TAKE OVER THE WORLD?

OH, YES... A SLEIGH OF COURSE!

FAIR ENOUGH... OFF YOU POP.

OH, BUT THERE *IS* ONE THING I SHOULD PROBABLY MENTION...

AAAARGH! *WHAT?!*

I HAVE SOME OF YOUR FRIENDS HERE...

THE UNICORN WAS A BONUS!

*HE'S GOING TO TAKE OUR MEMORIES!*

OKAY, YOU JUST RUINED MY BIG EVIL REVEAL!

WHO EVEN IS THAT?

NO IDEA...

IT'S ME, NEILL!

NEILL!

ANYWAY, *AS I WAS SAYING...*

USING MY STATE-OF-THE-ART WIRE-LESS TECHNOLOGY, I'VE SYNCED YOUR MEMORY ERASER WITH MY VERY OWN MEMORY-WIPER RIGHT *HERE...*

SO *THAT* WAS WHAT THE SYNCING WAS!

AS SOON AS YOU ACTIVATE *YOUR* MEMORY ERASER ON THE WORLD LEADERS, IT'LL AUTOMATICALLY ACTIVATE THIS ONE *HERE...*

ON YOUR FRIENDS.

*WHAT?!* NO!

WHAT DO YOU CARE?!

YOU'LL HAVE THE *WORLD!* EVIL EMPEROR PENGUIN DOESN'T NEED FRIENDS TO RULE THE WORLD... *DOES HE?*

**LATER...**

SO, THERE'S THIS CAT WHO IS MY ARCH-NEMESIS, AND HE IS ALWAYS FOILING MY EVIL PLANS....

HE'S NOW HOLDING NUMBER 8, EUGENE, KEITH AND THAT-ONE-WITH-THE-GLASSES HOSTAGE. AND IF I TAKE OVER THE WORLD, THEY'LL NEVER REMEMBER EVER KNOWING ME...

ALL THE MEMORIES GONE... JUST LIKE THAT.

I MEAN, WORLD DOMINATION IS ALL I'VE EVER WANTED! AND THIS IS MY CHANCE TO FINALLY HAVE IT!

WHAT SHOULD I DO? WHAT WOULD *YOU* DO, DASHER?!

LOOK, MATE, MY DEGREE IS IN SLEIGH-PULLING, NOT MENTORING VILLAINS.

I CAN'T LET ANYONE GET IN MY WAY! *I'M DOING THIS!*

C'MON, RUDOLPH, GUIDE US TO OUR FIRST STOP...

THE QUEEN OF ENGLAND!

I'M GLAD YOUR EVIL MASTER ACCIDENTALLY ONCE MADE A BIG RED BUTTON THAT SUMMONED ME.

HAHA, HE NEVER DID LIKE YOU, KEITH.

HE NEVER LIKED ME EITHER.

I DON'T THINK HE LIKES ANY OF US REALLY...

BUT THAT'S WHAT WE LOVE ABOUT EVIL EMPEROR PENGUIN. HE DISLIKES US FROM THE HEART.

HEY! STOP REMINISCING! WHAT'S THE POINT?! YOU'LL FORGET IT ALL ANY TIME NOW ANYWAY...

YOU'RE JUST JEALOUS, BECAUSE YOU'VE GOT NO FRIENDS! AND EVIL MASTER IS AMAZING!

WE'LL REMEMBER AS MUCH AS WE WANT UNTIL WE LOSE OUR MEMORIES!

GIFTZAP!

GOLLY!

REMEMBER WHEN I HELPED EVIL MASTER FOR A DAY AND THE EVIL BASE EXPLODED?

AND THE TIME YOU LAUNCHED ALL OF HIS CANS OF SPAGHETTI HOOPS INTO SPACE!

GIFTZAP!

REMEMBER THE TIME EVIL MASTER GOT CHASED BY A HUNKY VIRUS INSIDE A COMPUTER?!

HAHA! THAT WAS A GOOD ONE... AND WHEN YOU AND SIR GOT TURNED INTO BABIES!

GIFTZAP!

GIFTZAP!

I REMEMBER WHEN EVIL MASTER WENT LOOPY BECAUSE HIS SPAGHETTI HOOPS GOT STOLEN!

GIFTZAP!
GIFTZAP!
GIFTZAP!
GIFTZAP!
GIFTZAP!
GIFTZAP!
GIFTZAP!
GIFTZAP!
GIFTZAP!
GIFTZAP!
GIFTZAP!

HE SAID HE'D ABOLISH TUESDAYS IF HE TOOK OVER THE WORLD... AND CROISSANTS.

I THINK HE SECRETLY LOVES MY RAINBOWS...

HE ALWAYS CALLED ME A SQUID EVEN THOUGH I'M AN OCTOPUS...

HE CALLED ME A BIG TOE ONCE...

58

MEMORY ERASER ACTIVATED... READY FOR INITIATION.

ANY MOMENT NOW! HEEE-HEEEEE!

THREE HOURS LATER...

WHAT'S TAKING HIM SO LONG?!

SURELY HE'D BE ON THE MOON BY NOW!

MY PLANS CHANGED...

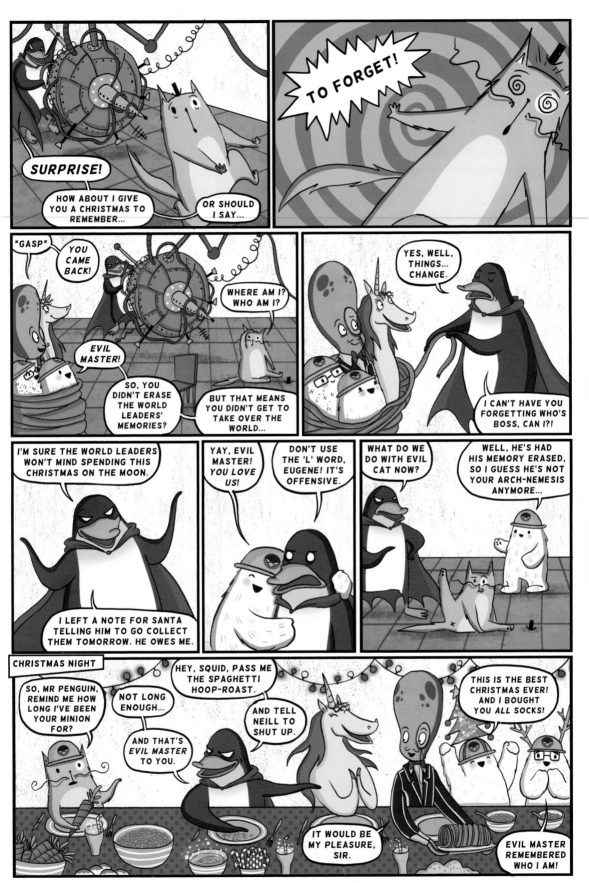

# MONITORING THREE MORE EEP BOOKS ↴

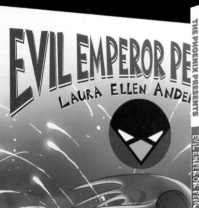

OBSERVE WEBSITE ADDRESS:

www.thephoenixcomic.co.uk

YOUR AMAZING WEEKLY COMICS ARE BEING HELD HOSTAGE. IF YOU EVER WISH TO READ THEIR INCREDIBLE PAGES AGAIN, THEN VISIT THE WEBSITE BELOW...

WWW.THEPHOENIXCOMIC.CO.UK

# the PHOENIX
### THE WEEKLY STORY COMIC